GLASGOW
kisses

To Noel, Amy and Katie

GLASGOW
kisses
x x

Valentines from the classroom

Published 2010 by Waverley Books Ltd,
144 Port Dundas Road, Glasgow, G4 0HZ, Scotland

Text © Nora Naughton 2010

ISBN 978 1 84934 012 0

WAVERLEY
BOOKS

Printed and bound in Poland.

Preface

The idea for this compilation of Valentine verses has been forming in my mind for a long time. Before the appeal of commercial Valentine cards, in Glasgow and its environs, the Valentine preparations and celebrations started in January. All around Glasgow, cards would be created and decorated with made-up rhymes. Many a class at school was disrupted by the swapping of pieces of paper with more and more outrageous rhymes, with much giggling and sniggering!

Whether you sent a card to yourself, to ten boys, to your sister or to your friends to play tricks on them, the fun was in the making and watching the reactions of people on the 14th and 15th February as they laughed about the rhymes and tried to guess who had sent them.

As part of our social history, it is important that these are not lost. While compiling them, a group of us had a great time as we 'walked down memory lane' remembering the lucky people who were sent the cards and the postmen who must have been entertained by the envelopes.

So, treat yourself to a rare wee trip down memory lane and enjoy! Remember who sent them to you and where you sent your cards and how much fun you had.

And if you are of an age when you are beginning to think about sending your first Valentine card, I hope this compilation will inspire you to create some new verses of your own!

Nora Naughton

In the parlour there were three,
You, the standard lamp and me.
Two's company, three's a crowd,
So the standard lamp went out!

Look under the table, look under the lamp,
You'll find my name under the stamp!

My heart is like a cabbage
Carefully halved in two.
The leaves I give to others,
The heart I give to you.

Written in ink,
Sealed with a kiss,
I love the boy
Who opens this.

The sun makes heat,
Rain makes a puddle.
What's a kiss
Without a cuddle?

Somebody loves you, somebody cares,
Your name is whispered in
somebody's prayers.
All day long, all day through,
Somebody's heart is longing for you.

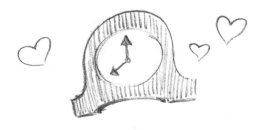

I loved you once,
I love you still,
I always have,
I always will.

I love you, I love you, I love you almighty,
I wish your pyjamas were next to my nightie.
Don't be mistaken, don't be misled,
I mean on the clothesline and not in the bed!

My love for you will never fail,
I carry it round in a wee tin pail!

When God was giving out good looks,
There was a big, long queue.
I was in the middle, dear,
But where on earth were you?

Lovely to look at,
   Lovely to see,
Not you, ya daftie!
I'm referring to me.

If kissing was against the law
And hugging was a crime,
I'd gladly spend my life with you
In Barlinnie doing time.

Beer is beer,
Whisky is whisky,
Goin' with you
Is awfy risky.

A ring is round — so is a shilling,
I am ready if you are willing.

Please don't be angry with this card,
To win your heart I've tried so hard.
And when you're with a girl that's new,
Just remember I love you.

Water is water,
Wine is wine,
A kiss from you
Would be divine.

Postie, Postie,
Hurry! Hurry!
Maybe he'll take me for a curry!
(Hint! Hint!)

Postie, Postie,
Run like mad.
This'll cheer him up
If he feels sad!

Postie, Postie,
Do your duty,
Take this to my
Blue-eyed beauty.

Postie, Postie,
If you see him,
Tell him that
I'll never leave him.

Roses are red,
Violets are blue,
Honey is sweet
And so are you.

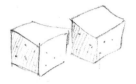

Roses are red,
Violets are blue,
Sugar is sweet,
What happened to you?

Roses are red,
Buttercups are yellow,
I'll be your girl
If you'll be my fellow.

Roses are red,
Violets are blue,
Even Dracula
Is nicer than you.

Roses are red,
Shamrocks are green,
My face might be funny
But yours is a scream.

You've hair like Elvis
And eyes like Presley too,
But when it comes to kissing,
You taste like Irish stew!

I'd visit you in China,
I'd visit you in Spain,
I'd visit you in Barlinnie,
If you go in again.

It wasn't at a party,
It wasn't at a dance,
It was at school
That I first found romance.

Last night I dreamt a dream,
A dream that made me laugh.
I dreamt that I was bubbles of soap
Floating in your bath.

Cupid shot an arrow
Right up into the sky.
Instead of landing in my heart,
It landed in my eye.

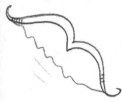

Cupid shot an arrow,
He shot it in reverse.
Instead of landing in my heart,
It landed in my *rse!

I like sugar, I like tea,
I like you, do you like me?
I like cake, I like jam,
If you want me, here I am.

Look	and	that	but	you	then	will
Up	you	I	if	love	all	be
And	will	love	you	me	my	for
Down	see	you,	find	not,	love	got.

Marriage is not a word,
It's a sentence.

I ran up the door and opened the stairs,
I said my pyjamas and put on my prayers,
I turned off the bed and jumped into the lights,
All because I kissed you goodnight!

From a flame . . .
. . . to a flame,
Who the blazes sent it?

I had a heart and it was true,
But now it's gone from me to you.
So guard it well as I have done,
For you have two and I have none.

Someone who's in love with you
Is sending you this card,
She is faithful and true to only you,
To win your love, she's tried so hard.

My dearest one in this sweet way my heart I offer you,

You captivate me every day in all you say and do.

Will you be my Valentine? I do implore say 'yes',

For nothing in this whole wide world, could bring more happiness.

There is nothing half so dear
As love's sweet song,
And ever since the time we met,
I dream the whole day long
Of joys I'd bring to you, my dear,
If only you were mine.
So please accept this card from me
And be my Valentine.

Your hair is straight,
Your legs are bandy,
But never mind,
They'll come in handy.

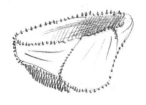

When we get married,
We'll have twins.
You buy the nappies,
And I'll buy the pins!

I passed your window,
I saw you undress,
A wee woolly shirt,
A wee string vest.
I could have seen more
But fate was unkind,
You came to the window
And pulled down the blind.

Two can live as cheap as one,
Or so the saying goes.
But who would live with a guy like you,
Heaven only knows!

If Cupid knew how happy
He could make me today,
I'm sure he'd take an arrow
And shoot it straight your way.
So now I'm truly hoping
He'll make our hearts combine,
By getting you to say
That always you'll be mine.

Knickers are red,
Knickers are blue,
If you don't love me,
Knickers to you!

Under the moonlight,
Under the roses,
But the best place to kiss
Is under the noses!

kiss
here

Postie, Postie,
Ring the bell.
If her dad answers,
Run like hell!

H O L L A N D

Hope
Our
Love
Lasts
And
Never
Dies

ITALY

I'll
Truly
Always
Love
You

Oh, I love you
Or so you think.
But deep down,
I think you stink!

I think you're so lovely,
I'd like to cuddle you.
To me you're someone special,
I hope I am to you.

Love is like a golden chain
Which brings two hearts together,
And if you ever break this chain,
You'll break my heart forever.

I wish I was a cigarette,
Rolled up nice and neat,
And every time you took a puff,
Our lips would surely meet!

_____ I love you,
  I do.
_____ I need you,
  be true.

Love is just a little word,
The letters are just four.
If I tried with all my heart,
I couldn't love you more.

Some love one,
Some love two.
I love one
And that one's you.

A ring is round,
A box is square.
Wouldn't we make
A happy pair?

I wish I was a little shoe
And you a piece of leather,
And some old cobbler would come along
And stitch us both together.

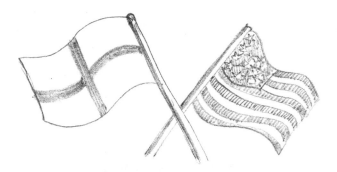

American boys are handsome,
English boys are sweet,
But it takes a boy from Glasgow
To sweep me off my feet!

If all the boys lived over the sea,
What good swimmers girls would be!

Peaches grow in Florida,
They grow in Australia too,
But it takes a place like
                    Pollokshields

To grow a peach like you!

I love you in the morning
And in the evening too,
And when I go to sleep to dream,
I always dream of you.

Postie, Postie,
Do your stuff,
And take this to
My wee cream puff.

Postie, Postie
Don't be slow.
Go like Elvis,
Go man go!

Postie, Postie,
Do not tarry.
Take this to
The one I'll marry.

Postie, Postie,
Fly like a dove,
And take this to
The one I love.

My dearest, darling heart's delight,
I dreamt a dream of you last night.
I dreamt that you beside me lay
But when I woke it was a flea!

Last week I saw you at a sale,
Buying a shirt without a tail,
A 10p tie and a 20p vest,
And, oh my goodness, you think
you're dressed!

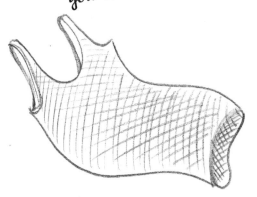

Ashes to ashes,
Dust to dust.
I'd kiss you now
But my lips would rust.

I don't want the moon or the stars above,
All I long for is your love.

I wish I were an angel
Watching you from above,
Then I would be able to find
The one you really love.

Your kiss is dying on my lips,
The last one that you gave me.
The doctors say I'm fading fast,
And another one would save me!

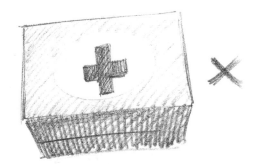

I wish I were a china cup
From which you drank your tea,
And every time you took a sip,
You'd be kissing me.

It's bad to lose a towel
When your eyes are full of soap,
But it's even worse to lose the one you love
When your heart is full of hope.

Hearts 2 United 1
(Junior results later)

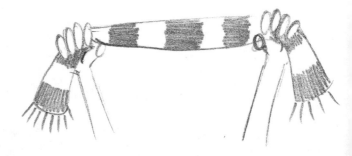

When Cupid shoots his arrow,
  He very seldom misses.
And when he hits his target,
He makes a Miss, a Mrs!

A ring is round,
It has no end.
To win your heart,
I do intend.

I do believe the Lord above
Created you for me to love.
He picked you out from all the rest,
Because He knew I loved you best.

From an onion
To a pickle,
How about
Some slap and tickle?

The little things you say and do,
Make me so in love with you.

A ring is round,
A well is deep.
Without your love
I cannot sleep.

Rose are red,
Violets are blue,
A face like yours
Belongs in a zoo.

Boys annoy me,
That is true.
There's only one exception
And that is you.

Maybe it was Cupid's dart that hit this heart of mine,
  For when I set my eyes on you I said 'My Valentine'.
You see I'd loved you quite a while but never dared to say,
  'Will you be my Valentine from this very day?'

When this card is yellow with age
And the words that I've written dim on the page,
Remember me kindly and do not forget,
Wherever you are, I'll remember you yet.

_ _ _ _ _ is a good boy,
He goes to church on Sunday.
He prays to God to give him strength
To kiss me on the Monday.

If I go to Heaven but you're not there,
I'll carve your name on a golden stair.
If you're not there on Judgement Day,
I'll know you've gone the other way.
And just to show my love is true,
I'll even go to Hell for you.

Postie, Postie,

_ _ _ _ _ _'s so thin,

You might be mistaken

And think he's not in!

Jingle, jangle,
Bingle, bangle,
You look good
From every angle.

From a devil . . .
. . . to a devil.
Who the devil sent it?

When God was giving out good looks,
You must have been in his good books.

♡   ♡   ♡   ♡   ♡   ♡

G.I. love you.
G.I. do.
G.I. want to.
G.I. do.

Music is music,
A dance is a dance.
What is love
Without romance?

East is east,
West is west,
You're the boy
That I love best.

Celtic Green,
Rangers Blue,
Hearts United,
Me + You.

Beware of girls with eyes of brown,
They kiss you once then let you down.
Beware of girls with eyes of blue,
They kiss you once then ask for two!

Forget the writing,
Forget the blot.
But, my darling,
Forget me not.

Two in a hammock,
Trying to kiss,
Trying to be funny,
Ending up like SIHL.

Peas and beans
  Fill the ladle.
  But I need you
  To fill the cradle.

If you'll be my secret passion,
I'll share with you my sweetie
ration.

Ashes to ashes,
Dust to dust,
I hope you're a boy
A girl can trust.

Water is water,
Tide is tide.
What's a groom
Without a bride?

We tried it on the sofa,
We tried it on the chair,
We tried it in the garden,
We couldn't do it there.
We tried it on the windowsill,
And, oh, it was a laugh
To see how many times we tried
To take a photograph!

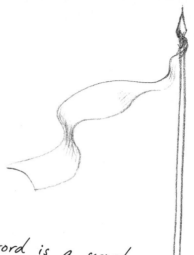

A sword is a sword,
A lance is a lance,
And when you kiss me
I go into a trance.

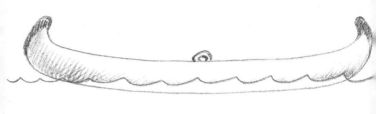

Love many,
Trust few.
Always paddle
Your own canoe.

Down by the river,
Carved on the rocks,
Three little words,
'Forget me not'.

Down by the river,
Carved on a tree,
Three little words,
'I love thee'.

The boy who makes a promise,
The boy who never can,
The boy who breaks a promise,
Will never make a man.

Three rings:
Engagement – ring,
Wedding – ring,
Suffer – ring!

I wrote this Valentine in jest,
Not to offend you, I've tried my best,
And who it's from, you've probably guessed.
Oh! This rhyme's a bit of a pest,
I can't think of any more words
Ending in 'est'.

Every time I hear your name,
Deep inside I feel a pain.
To myself I put this question:
Is it love or indigestion?

Although you do not love me,
Although you do not care,
If you ever need me,
I will always be there.

Two in the bed and the bed was rocking,
Under the blankets the sight was shocking.
Don't be mistaken and don't be misled,
It's only two brothers fighting in bed!

Ham is ham,
Veal is veal.
What's a kiss
Without a feel?

I must not say I want you or wish
that you were mine.
I must not say I love you or
show you any sign.
I must not let my eyes light up each time
I hear your name.
You're someone else's boyfriend but
I love you just the same!

Written with love,
Sealed with a kiss.
I love the boy
Who opens this.

Roses are red,
Violets are blue,
I'm feeling quite desperate
So you'll have to do.

Postie, Postie,
Do not falter.
This may lead me
To the altar!